Y0-BOI-881

HOURGLASS TRANSCRIPTS

By the same author:

Spelt (with Myung Mi Kim), San Francisco, CA: a+bend press, 1999

Black Box Cutaway, Berkeley, California: Kelsey Street Press, 1998

Prosthesis : : Caesarea, Elmwood, Connecticut: Potes and Poets Press, 1994 (limited edition of 30 copies)

Taken Place, London & Cambridge: Reality Street Editions, 1993

Linen minus, Bolinas, California: Avenue B Press, 1992

Domino: point of entry, Buffalo, New York: Leave Books, 1992

Narrative's Journey: The Fiction and Film Writing of Dorothy Richardson, New York, New York: Peter Lang Publishing, 1995

811.54
G337

SUSAN GEVIRTZ

Hourglass Transcripts

WITHDRAWN

Burning Deck, Providence
2001

LIBRARY ST. MARY'S COLLEGE

The author wishes to thank the editors of the following journals where sections of this book first appeared: *Aufgabe, Primary Writing, Outlet, St Mark's Poets and Poems, Prosodia, Proliferation, Crayon,* and the anthology: *NewWritings on Motherhood and Poetics,* Patricia Dienstfrey and Brenda Hillman, eds., University of California Press (forthcoming).

Burning Deck is the literature program of Anyart: Contemporary Arts Center, a tax-exempt non-profit corporation.

Cover by Keith Waldrop

© 2001 by Susan Gevirtz
ISBN 1-886224-40-4, original paperback
ISBN 1-886224-41-2, original paperback, 50 signed copies

LIBRARY ST MARY'S COLLEGE

For David, Clio and Zaid

CONTENTS

RESUSCITATIONS   9

HOLLOWED OUT BOOK   15

SYLLABARY DISPOSSESSION   35

THE HOURGLASS TRANSCRIPTS 51

RESUSCITATIONS

arm leg kindling gather where water blankets sound take her
down again again quiet crown

was strong singing you swimming practicing breathing
stripmining the superfluous

to anything recalled ever to everything ever summoned the
former a project of the former

sea fence Sea Gate said promise of plenty said gather greens of
tomorrow mainland winds mountain up once every 4,200 seconds

from lucid sea like none ever witnessed abbreviation the
situation engineered a couldn't say (or far worse

and so tending to every and none seeing not saying bluntly a
management preoccupation in familiar waters

carefully considered beginning rests with the rest turning away
turns the turned

what is the meaning of the word *lagoon* what a tribute that you're
all still here sweet nothings

warm in flannel under the ground "here's what we'll do —
when you sleep I'll sleep, when you wake up I'll wake up"

a long way to Tipperary to the place by the ocean its fishermen
and fine sand see the crypt correcting herself

land owners want land boat owners want bones boats want
shortwave sound wants bait land lies in wait

someone was behind her also a man was near pointing "You're
still there" unable to name or swim panting

between finger and singer machine's refrain between teeth the
difference

crosshairs correcting the spiral of wandering attention's
gunscope once I arrived landscape's low status slow statues

of noise no promise longer than sea's sleep that never rests short
of words over over sent

stick figure swaddled in chain mail escape hatch unlocks picture
postcards finger's touch

by sea's preface before the world was faceless now her face take
swallows silence soon down

the word regret the word repent whiplash on halved horizon be-
headed by halves the almost left holds hope behind right's back

belies the way face belies fact an act to cover the desire for never
achieved or relation to idea as act

wound or sunken awoken profile proximity's imposition face on
face of

and at our last parting last words I promised enfolded routing in
the gulf offing

written in caterpillar scar constellation written in rain star launch
reserves literally last week's facsimilie face used up

plenaria aria axis belief voids all attempts sent to preliminary
galaxy beyond belief's chair

—For Clio
—For Helen

HOLLOWED OUT BOOK

I look therefore I conceal
                    —Robbe-Grillet

N O L

portage

backwards

through

the book

Tributary

Arbitrary

seen from afar
seen as affront

deep plotting
dense carpeting
coming going
of those who
come to go

HANJIN

"...."   "easily misreads us

seems to intricate

to unwind us"

         dyspathy on board
         so the billiards
         become vineyards and all
         passengers sink
         into the impossible light
         moat of surround sound

The First Syllable of NOVEMBER

. . . upon the captive sky
—Ovid

foretold
into   into
turns

the end hears
bird and also flame
        for this line

        no hope
        for this

        time

    twists her ankle on what she heard while

    he trips over what she saw

      as on as on

into foreclosed

of hope's

captive

sold

skyward

the caught
hears

the found

HYUNDAI

Forever alter the ellipse of one night

decision unannounced, lips busy

Chapter ten means to get away from   but their faces take
the hero's place   on the place of tomorrow
album spread
or her open
              in place of sight

the subject Veronica chased by memory   In order to understand
we must outline, even spell: a letter can always be missing can
open the bay
in the word   can
outlive

or may freeze up

where the grapher trains the auto

At their whim she
can appear again in order
to remind them that they are

dressed as if
in question
she can be
on call
[because the word is fertile
it is spacing my love you
my evil scriptural double breasted
activity   meanwhile she can just as well
make the alphabet err:

knowing where the next meal comes from
the image respects its echo

knowing who will be the next meal

half way between written tides and diatribes

not a question of what came

first read the things
on the shelf First the objects
as reprises, responses the sentence
they are

The Annexes

Aspiration or Exorcism
    This is an example of strong intermuscularity
        a choice must be
        or a check written

animated sand
sparkle ceiling
star-studded shore
on to which one step

under gravel pitted sky
the underwater moves
the generous silence
                invitations
                to wait
                in line to wake up

Why the white of uniform
is such a long white?

Or the building edge so sharp   it slices at
the night

winter   this long misconstruance
of what could
be light

The Right of Inspection

I have had I keep I have
—Césaire

before after

(same question the same old question)

In the days when
we were always always

a stained glass window
jig saw puzzle
half fur half skin
She
fire burning fire
"to regain my faith in flame" —Ruiz

went on a voyage to cast out
interruption
first this then
that oceanliner
at a distance so close
the crew could converse
through closed windows
across the bay
infant's horizon
vast unborn up close

Then the vincible invisible presents himself. "It's possible to be immune to landscape," he says, "and in the next few hours I will demonstrate to you: World Under the World but not the Underworld" — a place you can visit like Florida and then return

    dot   air   spark   eat fire   burn ash

while the earth is still

    soft

IMEDIA

many entrances
many embraces entrance us

epilepsy of kiss   epistolary in which

["I'm the product of your wishes"]

Make amedia dialogue   quote or
hands a quiet talk
Make a disappointing
sentence

The short haired verb or to show her interest

reportage

That   the sentence   the runaway   runway from which
took off   the sentence was saying directions and   diction the
same flowering annunciation

At The Sign of the Pause

...: burn in ambivalence

    repeating itself cancels itself

This is the causeway "Time Gone By"
that cause built

This the

assassinated name
assassin of name
remains
white on beige
wall

illumination beyond recognition

A camera strapped to a pigeon or
the airplanes that "...threw bombs, like a lightening flash, to
illuminate the earth for a photo." —Kaja Silverman

This is the

like modern planes that fly underwater and take off
from air

This

12 Seconds of Then

boarding for a tour of the archipelageo from An Cephaly to Spina Bifida, next Santa Kidney, Saint Trysome, then through the Placental Lake region and resting for a day on San Downs

The camera comes to a stop on a woman standing twenty or thirty years to the left of the man in the trench coat

        imaginary anatomy
        nautical map
        by which they travel
        at night
        making safe harbor of themselves
        or themselves

MAERSK

...: The distance needed to portray

"I will never forget" quiet world filled with sound therefore
are you sure you went...?

The tired plot
sleeping in its cabin

 ...: overboard
clauses and dice
retrieved with a net
sardines fly through
red hoops

M, the heroine of course
X, the stranger, and A, we know absoultely nothing about
One making a suggestion the other resisting
as if that is how it has always been

"the music has gradually been transformed into a man's voice.
This voice speaks continuously, but although the music has
stopped completely, we cannot yet understand the words."
—Robbe-Grillet

X's voice: Once again—   once again
candlelight on an oceanliner is
a woman's bedtime story
overthrown overthrown

the tired pilot   the sleeping plot

as if
over

O * C L

"...an action under the stipulation would not lie, as a person unable to speak could not stipulate." —Agrippa

What kind of calumny it was
what kind of complaint I have chosen
to discuss at a later date
And so now having returned to this country

                            (or century)

I will keep my word
A fake princess, the understudy of all girls,
will be my premise

              (or promise)

We argue from the interpretation of a name
the demonstration as it glides
by on the sea's surface

as so much wind makes the landscape
stand still
in motion

        empty headed
        empty headed
        how better you
        speak the book of the world
           (or pass through
              that canal)

E V E R G R E E N: "Assasins of Memory"

—Vidal-Naquet

Human hair bales

display harvest

a hank of hair and a jar full of ashes
does not a wedding make

WESTERN BULK

Space is a frame up
 we fill ourselves
 in   the skull   full

bees   on a summer day

                              honeycomb
                              eyesockets

                              the sight

                              this honey

ANZDL

the flirtationists   decapitated by industry   marry

members of the jury

bodily harm's
burden of proof
shadowing reason   Names of those strolling

the deck   without regret

the 700 things I could say doze
cut cheese with a stick
find the limitations of the eye
and flatter flatten   those seahorses missed
          as they gallop by

the lung of our masters
we are required to acquire proficiency
not merely radios   not mere
access
land acts   trust acts   but on what stage and while turning
we turn into what cargo?

A R C O / C O S C O

the system of script   too dry for the ink

within the sore throat
of a system of control

Accelerated holding in place
comes loose the character dictates

Again surround sound
scattered to the four winds

collected here in a funnel

   commune
consuming vision   pinned

   the profile mistake
of the profile viewing   itself

for itself
the ending you want will
   not What is it you still
       expect to happen

               There must be long distance calls
               danger of losing track
               topiary of cement

               and I took your hand or
               was it your

               garden at night
               your cement sea

D S R - SENATOR . . . : *"flipbook"*

The shoals were thin that year

The pillars sickened into sugar

as we passed

the harbour silted up

No one could

cry no one

could inhale until

our gills came back

then under was upper

flutter was the rampant whisper

which we tried to catch

casting fish-hooks

at the skies

Here where the first quinqueremes sailed I
saw far beneath
my feet the breakwater
of the ancient harbour

blindly
binding
body to body
thin sliver of thin air

built of skin trespassed
on feet of metal
celestial speak up   map of read-me-to-sleep
the contrary context of "next-to-next"
Two girls on one swing
where cry is spelled   *city*   eventually

at our last parting she said
"when your body is born"
tracing paper launches the barge

lie down
dwarf of passage
everything is present
                    [TH
            promised to visibility
          you

            why the ocean

            doesn't overflow

            How the wind

            howls

            and other rhymes
            you'll arrive

            knowing

            then   a life
               these songs   their answers
            you'll forget

Syllabary Dispossession

of watered stone   of piled stone   of raked stone made
of made of made up   wouldn't wouldn't
couldn't   One ate stone

Part rasp part file this the tool found in the empty
house   Telling   shadow in the doorway   magnet — and I
extended my arms three times
to take her   again she whimpers:
the restriction
of the final word

Tqllßarenry wlaꞇ·ꞺꜲcc ꝺeevꞏnꜹrd... ꞻ nꞮeꞏꝺowꞓꞃuꞇꝃꞆꝺ ꝉ·ꝺ aꞃ·ꞃꞇꞇꞄsꞄꞮꞓꞇꞃ

The founding

first   second third

Tqllßarenry wlaꞇ·ꞺꜲcc ꝺeevꞏnꜹrd... ꞻ nꞮeꞏꝺowꞓꞃuꞇꝃꞆꝺ ꝉ·ꝺ aꞃ·ꞃꞇꞇꞄsꞄꞮꞓ the fantasmatic   foundling

first first and too late

Where there are

here are

Here falls

From there

Dead numbers   818 762 3878   empty bed

spinners fly   gouting flames

the Hades landscape or Ridley's inferno

"His score became a major character"
the soul of the soul survives survival: Expiation:

> "Apparently there had been death... The...lowering of
> blank skies."

"Apparently that had bee death The lowering of blank skies" re ing is magnet

Palace Ex

cursus   excursion

First lines
first
lines then

trapdoor   conundrum
reversible sentences

phone perforations "so our errors" err
You might want to hum this "heir" the
appearance of resemblance the impression
"hair" style of pretence practiced by all
"all" all our heirs the inside-out of air

It is

Not now

never now

It is   Always now

only now

It is It is It is

Here sits

the way the way

falling

away

where one someone says "the results were three-fold; the first two a
mineral and kelp the third necessary element for health was ecstasy" a
fact derived from the air at open sea

Thalacy you with th black piano h'ni une hanor tla th reah d boon day

    moon caught in the clock

     and laughing through it

    broken teeth

      numbers drawn

      lotto sleep

      So back you

      float table   chair   cushion   vase

        permanent's

          impermanent place

The low skies with the black sun shining. Apparently
there had been day:

Always falls

the fall

of the house of always

house falls

away

away falls
the fall
away of always

miles of days

Ex minutes   to the meeting of Ex
and one since the last sighting

outlast yourself last

visitation refused
look elsewhere
to rock
your face

22 ways to fall
away all fall

For each month a house   and for each house
    a waterfall   Each house a day's walk apart

and each footstep on the alpine trail activates the next waterfall
as the one behind ebbs with the back of departure

          Each house, a month

              calendar based

      on the waterfall year

           part Hollywood   part Hawaii

           part round

           part smoke

      (burn in retribution) one smokey cavity where one month was

back lit. Depicted as under an arc of light. Shining like wet — a
glance-point like off glass slippers. Glitter that won't wash off. The
couple installed in their opera box wearing (Freud's) cap of hearing.
So each aria is exultant love cash. Won't wash wears off over years

                Tⱥⱡlʋɪɪʀᴇ˙ⱳⱳⱳⱱ ⱬꙅˑɴɩaᴣꜱɪɪᴇɩ

a soft perenial hand grenade
what I meant
aloft the bouyant blue without relent

One arm pinned

to the chest

like a pin wears his arm

This one is named the

but won't tell

throw   feed it
hands reversible sentences the phantom of a concept and
the like
this writing
like writing then
the hungry river memory
of motion

Piracy you radiant chateau

the warming of stars

expiation in the hand thrown heat

Primacy you radiant star. Expiation in the hand in hand
heat:

back of it of there was hander to arc though to min fig are wet and

A nurse is seen to kiss a soldier on a bench in the park. The baby
develops a sore in its mouth — the disgusting development is a
lapse of time.
"This is one example and it will suffice"   The body of the
film however, massages hope   A vision
of horror can remain forever
A census of psyches   so to speak   fear of a thing
does not expel that thing
suffer at the hands of little children or circumstance:
uprorarious delight

The audible girl. Three masters, one servant, one winged sprite
in the mud   ice   water   fire

> turning turning the round basin
> in his hands [Atlas, so to speak;
> the world, so to speak:] the servant
> finds gold.
>   Analogy Allegory Allergy   Thunderstorm of penury

where I first began with the uncanny
icy burial   the birthday incident — "a pendulum stroke
in the empty arctic air"

"the word after"   the word
after the last spoken
to say the word beyond
the last

Rotten Rope

Gold Nuggets

Muddy Blackness

panchromatic ". . . and this impossibility of escape is repeated in
another way when he has returned just as the waves must have
something to break on

heart stopped
in the watch or
strapped
to it Two endings
fastened two
endings panning

as The House of Fans meets The House of Glasses
as The House of Fans VERSUS The House of Glasses

as one House cuts the other story wrestles between its end

postcard obscenities innocently beckoning pretend

    inside the postcard

    small craft circling circling
            circling

on the ground
  circling
circling the air
circling circling

          This This

        This

        is

       this what

       this that

       can be
       taken
       this

       the

taken

away take the taken away

                                                                lhskɑlʊɪᴦɪɐᴧɪsᴄu

                                                                        drank yourself

                                                                down

                                                past legibility   into sleep's

past

this
what's
left
take

take

                Uncertain derivation

                dissyllable disoluble

So go

  gone

on to one

go trot

go

on

give rise
give heat
eat stone
give bread

where gone go
off run

THE HOURGLASS TRANSCRIPTS

HYPHEN'S HYPHEN

Nothing is thought

or what we
thought

I stayed out of your body

to let it air

but the air would not

I stayed out of the air

to let the body

but avail
not

The unopened room in which the tide had gone out exposing
miles of floor never before seen

Where there is everything

is never there

what in the world

susceptible to the call

to mean an order
                          it orders

hostage time

How continue
where there is no

outside

proximity's estuary

before
incident, arrival. Sojourn in matter. The sun's mind. Kymatik.
Isn't musical experience

outside sound's
light

drop song

a phenomenon keeps watch on itself

scouring the seabed

for unforseen

We enter the epoch

And nothing will stay stay

   nothing left

was

nothing

last

THERMOSTAT SONGS

Great distance embalming
great access   as if object
                          is the object

SONGS FOR SONG

— after Lorine Niedecker's
"Progression"

May will buy you flowers
   arrive at the door and
Give them to yourself
   May June me you July

   Great distance Great access As if Great: object
   Great distant access as if great object

How love happens coaxed from
the dark where sleep is an animal
wakeful and directionless

   Great distant access as if great objects

I typed all the miniatures into
   long-lined pages   I said the love
before the dark was dark
   I said before
now before is before before
and I not I

Great great is the great wild distance

lies in wait   can't
cup
cup too many
too bad too
actual place no place

Great great lies the great distant

This time eclipse of time
glissando you in the mirror
my account so far is
glare the unconscious in a well
bucket recite minerals
renewals animals

Great Great

Behind one apparent one
    who insists on the disappearant's
shadow larger gasp than any
    appearance could summon loom
looms the loom

Great no one No
And bought her flowers to hide her face in
    and the flowers by the bedside by the roadside
the flowers in the season of her mother's name
    and the flowers over her that blind her

Great

For each day centuries sent
    this bright world
This bright
    lobelia hibiscus grapevine jacaranda
world hand in hand the last
        sleep   sleep lattice
    Graze window of ever last
       strawberry   winter's idea
    the imagined's present

ICE AGE

of matter minus

matter minus matter

locked

on the way to

four punctures equal the paper path

roam

pestilant wolves
in pretend life

rats eat from birdfeeders

turn city

turn on soft feet

PERFIDIA

— for Frances Jaffer

How   maze

marauding   sleep's
                        shoreline

    little offering

where nothing can meet   proportion of what

    parsing gifts

nose dive two doves on a rail
preening each other's necks
under floodlight spring

wanting nothing more

while the closed mouth of

the book is hunger under

and the flowers that stand in for

UNDONE

recent memory there is no such which is

already there taxonomize you do

the three lives possessed replete struck

vocabulary of origin

always straight into the sun cannot

turn into recent memory

The silence was full of tone

shining it and wearing it as a wristwatch

Looking back all day it's been late

at night

CITY OF Ys

Not   the other

side of the world

couldn't care also

even this   anyone

about anything but cradling protecting walking around a thing
that had happened

Measure take measure this

world which side watches

which tent neighborhood
sense or planning fled

city of broken wrists

prehensile life's hope

here you too
temporarily housed
yet even under daylight
before umbrellas
they offered sun, mortar, one fat mole, wild honey
in a rush basket, eight minnows, a squirrel's broken tail

offered and offered

stalling a future making

a future unable to visit

the heavy sleeves of it

thus this cannot be your remains

you cannot remain you remind someone

the known crosses out

on the tray on which

withold itself lies but

the heard is not your concern

hungry foraging downstream

from the spot where

"black runs out of color" — Barbara Guest

and lost in invisible

landscape converts you

(who are not a who) on the bank

where water leaves one

city without

"...encountered on our doorstep a fellow who asked us the way to 'the lost city, the audacious city' ... I realize ... that by [this] he must mean the city of Ys." — Michel Leiris, 1944 Journal [The Liberation of Paris], translated by Lydia Davis, in *Conjunctions* 31, 1998.
"The city of Ys ... was a legendary city in Brittany said to have been swallowed up by the waves in the 4th or 5th century."—Lydia Davis

GRAVITY'S DEVOTIONS

—for Julie

The first insistance was coronation   hills of white

carnations jammed together like coincidence like audience at
the world series

Then talking nose to nose with the seal underwater she drops
the bowl and spoon which fall slowly and hit a rock making a
loud underwater noise

In the second insistance *of* and *at* arrive one carrying the other
on a stretcher the way a live ant carries a dead ant's body

The third insistance is coma. One side childhood, the other
trawling toward something else. Noon is the hour of the
sacrificial drinker of broth who for fourteen days did not use
the phone. To flee from the living to the more alive. Smog over
white roses on polished pine. Of two young shoplifting girls,
one would lie down so early

DEFERRAL

could provoke an event

cravenly

intermittent

something reporting

starved of light

close distance   will

close distance

DOMAIN

in the

we are

in

exists

irrevocable ravel

in we

are

Spring

in like

a room together

the unimaginable rest

of the house

the day's year

   won't let

us
out

someone else's

starved light

and the slow dentition of summer

slow here

gone

The perimeters of the room
   where the walls and floor meet
     are measure of hour
       time of year

The sky swallowing an airplane
she learns the sound of collapse
       involution wakeful
      the state
     of going by
     of being under as

      happened to
    ominous   voluminous having
  come out of fog   slower or later
last day or tomorrow   sooner comes also

the first touch lets the opponent know
or knows itself as before
touch

this explanation robs you this
explanation this addendum put
down your head   we to whom address
wavers in front of
veiled and bow
platters for the blind

FAR FAR AWAY

in a little wikkiup

no one could tell the difference

between space and hour

I said "wait" so you said "after"

One part is part of

the other is part at   and the other will always

remain always

as at first

sight

The orderlies have their instructions

and we   the instructions

have us   have us   preceed us   Outlive

and the artifactual animal

you wake to

SMCL

3 5151 00272 2965

This book was computer typeset in 10 pt. Palatino, with Zapf Chancery initials. Split lines curtesy of David Delp. Printed on 55 lb. Writers' Natural (an acid-free paper), smyth-sewn and glued into paper covers by McNaughton & Gunn in Saline, Michigan. Cover by Keith Waldrop. There are 750 copies, of which 50 are numbered and signed.